DISCARD

Dolphins
and Porpoises

DISCARD

DISCARD

Dolphins and Porpoises

DOROTHY HINSHAW PATENT

Holiday House

NEW YORK

J
599.53
P

51808

To the dedicated researchers who work to increase our understanding of these delightful creatures.

The author wishes to thank Dr. Louis M. Herman, Professor and Director of the Kewalo Basin Marine Mammal Laboratory at the University of Hawaii at Manoa, for reading and evaluating this book.

Copyright © 1987 by Dorothy Hinshaw Patent
All rights reserved
Printed in the United States of America
First Edition

Library of Congress Cataloging-in-Publication Data

Patent, Dorothy Hinshaw.
Dolphins and porpoises.

Includes index.
SUMMARY: A general introduction to dolphins and porpoises, highlighting such areas as individual species, life cycles, anatomy, feeding habits, sonar system, and social organization.
1. Dolphins—juvenile literature.   2. Porpoises—Juvenile literature.   [1. Dolphins.   2. Porpoises]
I. Title.
QL737.C432P38   1987   599.5'3   87-45332
ISBN 0-8234-0663-6

Contents

Dolphins
and Porpoises

Candice Cho is delighted to
sit on the back of a gentle
false killer whale, a kind of
dolphin. SEA LIFE PARK,
NICKI CLANCEY

1
Introducing Dolphins and Porpoises

DOLPHINS AND PORPOISES, THOSE PLAYFUL AND INTELLIGENT relatives of the great whales, have inspired special feelings in people for centuries. Many a ship that crossed the ocean has been accompanied along the way by dolphins riding the waves created by the bow. Since the time of ancient Greece, individual wild dolphins have voluntarily sought out human companionship, establishing real friendships. Ancient legends abound about dolphins making friends with people, especially young boys, even allowing them to ride upon their backs. While some people consider such stories merely myths, chances are there is truth to them. Dolphins in recent times have also acted in this way. A dolphin called Donald lived off the coast of Wales and Cornwall, England, in the 1970s. Donald would frolic with human divers, sometimes disrupting diving classes, and would tow boats and interfere with fishermen. Donald got bolder and bolder with time and even tried to carry off female divers on two occasions. Opo, a wild bottle-nosed dolphin in New Zealand in the 1950s, became very tame. He would come into shallow water and play with children, giving them rides on his back. Georgie Girl was a bottle-nosed dolphin in Florida that spent time with humans in the water. Even today, at Monkey Mia on the west coast of Australia, wild dolphins frolic with swimmers in the shallow waters.

As scientists and trainers work more and more closely with these curious and cooperative animals, they are often impressed by the animals' intelligence. Just how smart are dolphins, and how truly humanlike is their behavior? Such questions make us wonder if humans are really all that different from other living things.

WHAT ARE DOLPHINS AND PORPOISES?

Dolphins and porpoises are not fish. They are mammals, like dogs and cats. They are "warm-blooded"—that is, their bodies have ways of maintaining a constant warm temperature, even in the coldest water. Most mammals have a thick coat of fur that helps hold the warmth inside. But hair can slow down swimming, and dolphins and porpoises have none, except for a few bristles on the heads of some kinds. Instead of fur, these aquatic animals have a thick layer of fat called blubber under the skin, which helps keep their bodies warm. Unlike fish, mammals breathe air. Even though dolphins and porpoises spend their whole lives in the water, they must come to the surface often to take in air.

Dolphins and porpoises are members of the scientific order Cetacea, which includes all whales as well. While some whales lack teeth and filter their food from the water with huge sieves made of baleen, dolphins and porpoises are "toothed whales" (Odontoceti). Altogether, there are five families of toothed whales. Three of these contain only animals that are always called whales. One of the other toothed-whale families, called the Platanistidae, has five species, all called dol-

The killer whale shown here is a toothed whale that belongs to the same family as dolphins. STEPHEN MULLANE

The Amazon River dolphin belongs to the family Platanistidae. Notice its small eyes, large flippers, and flexible neck. STEINHART AQUARIUM

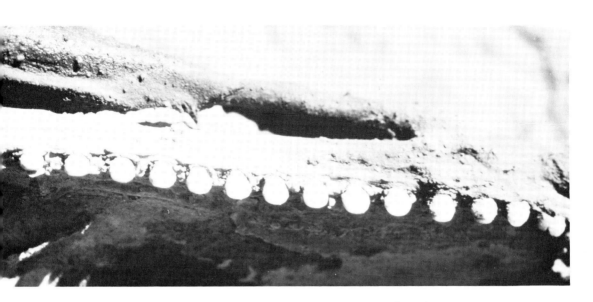
The spectacled porpoise has shovel-shaped teeth. © DOTTE LARSEN

phins, which live in rivers instead of in the sea. They have very small eyes or are blind, and have a long, thin beak and a bulging forehead. Their flippers are relatively large. Unlike those of other dolphins, all the vertebrae of their necks are separated rather than fused, so they can move their heads easily from side to side.

All the other animals called dolphins or porpoises belong to the family Delphinidae. Whether an animal is given the name *dolphin* or *porpoise* depends on who is talking. To most people, if the animal has a beak, it is a dolphin; if it lacks a beak, it is a porpoise. This is a fairly good rule, except that two species commonly called dolphins (the Irrawaddy dolphin and Risso's dolphin) have no beak to speak of.

Six other species without beaks are commonly called porpoises. While most scientists include porpoises in the family

Delphinidae, some put them in a separate family called the Phocoenidae. In addition to lacking a beak, these animals all have shovel-shaped teeth instead of the cone-shaped teeth of dolphins.

Another complicating factor in giving names to these animals is that six members of the family Delphinidae happen to be called whales.

Some scientists solve the problem simply by referring to all these animals as dolphins, since only six related species in the family Delphinidae are generally called porpoises. But still others prefer the word *porpoise* for all dolphins and porpoises. In this book, when describing general traits, the word *dolphin*

Dolphins have cone-shaped teeth. SEA LIFE PARK, MONTE COSTA

will be used. Particular kinds, however, will be called by their familiar common name, whether it is dolphin, porpoise, or whale.

A final source of confusion is two species of large fish that are sometimes called "dolphin" on restaurant menus. Other names for these tasty fish, which are preferred in order to avoid confusion with the true dolphin mammals, are mahi-mahi and dorado.

Getting Along in Water

Living in water requires a body quite different from that needed on land. The shiny dolphin body is shaped like a torpedo so that it glides smoothly through the water. No outside ears interfere with the body's sleek shape. The ears can only be seen as small holes just behind the eyes. Most kinds of dolphins have a dorsal fin along the back, which helps stabilize the body while the animal swims. At the rear is a special tail made up of two finlike flukes. While a fish's tail runs from top to bottom, a dolphin's tail sticks out on either side. This is because a swimming dolphin moves up and down, using powerful muscles to propel its body through the water, instead of moving from side to side like a fish. Dol-

Dall's porpoise NATIONAL MARINE MAMMAL LAB, NOAA

This white-sided dolphin has a very streamlined shape.
STEINHART AQUARIUM

The ear openings of these bottle-nosed dolphins are in the crease just behind their eyes. SEA LIFE PARK, MONTE COSTA

You can see the dorsal fin, left flipper, and the tail flukes of this leaping bottle-nosed dolphin. ALISA SCHULMAN

phins have one pair of flippers on their sides, where the front legs are on land mammals. The flippers keep the body balanced during swimming and can help steer. In close quarters, the flippers may be moved up and down to propel the animal slowly forward. The hind limbs have disappeared altogether during the long period of dolphin evolution, except for a couple of bones buried in the rear muscles.

The dolphin's "nose" is also quite different from that of a land animal. It is reduced to a blowhole on top of the head. When the animal surfaces, the blowhole opens and takes in air. When the dolphin goes under water, the blowhole closes so that water can't get in. The bottle-nosed dolphin breathes two to four times each minute when swimming near the surface, but it can hold its breath for seven minutes or more when diving. Some dolphins can dive very deep. Even though it usually lives in shallow water, the bottle-nosed dolphin has been trained to dive to 1,700 feet (518 meters). Scientists have observed a wild common dolphin voluntarily diving to 990 feet (302 meters), and pilot whales are known to dive to 2,000 feet (610 meters). When a dolphin breathes, almost all the air in its lungs is exchanged with fresh air so that its body can get as much oxygen as possible. The tissues of the body, too, can carry extra oxygen, which helps during long dives. Since the dolphin holds its breath when it dives and takes in no new air, it doesn't have a problem with "the bends"—nitrogen bubbles that form in the bloodstream of human divers who breathe compressed air while under water.

SENSING THE WORLD

We humans get most of our information about the outside world through our eyes. Hearing is also very important to us,

This mother bottle-nosed dolphin and her baby both have their blowholes open to take in air. MARINELAND OF FLORIDA

for it is through our ears that we do most of our day-to-day communicating. Our senses of smell and taste make our food interesting and give us some information about our environment, and our sense of touch aids us in many ways.

An animal living in the water needs different senses than one living on the land. We can figure out where we are by looking around us. Objects in our environment, such as trees, buildings, and signs, help us tell our location. In the water, however, there are fewer signposts. In the shallows, the features of the bottom may give some clues. But when the water isn't crystal-clear, it is hard to get information through vision. And since light doesn't penetrate very far in water, an animal deeper down can see little or nothing.

Sound travels through water about five times faster than through air, and it is carried for long distances. Whether the water is deep or shallow, sound penetrates it more reliably and farther than light. Since sound is so much more useful in water than light, it isn't surprising that dolphins rely on it for much of their information about the world around them.

These animals use sound in a very different way than we do. They don't just listen for the sounds made by things in the environment—they send out sounds of their own to tell what's out there. If you stand on the edge of a canyon and yell, your voice bounces back to you in an echo. You can tell approximately how far away the other side is if you count the seconds between your yell and the return of the echo. The farther away the opposite wall is, the longer it will take for your voice to return.

Dolphins use this echo principle to find their way about. But their echolocation, or sonar, system is quite complex. Dolphins give out a series of rapid clicks as they swim and listen for the returning clicks that have bounced off nearby objects. A dolphin may make as many as a hundred clicks each second. Dolphin sonar is very accurate and extremely sensitive. A dolphin can find an object as small as a BB using its sonar, and it can distinguish between a piece of copper and a piece of aluminum of the same size and thickness. In this way, dolphins "see" with their ears much as we do with our eyes.

Except for river dolphins, which live in such muddy water that eyes would be useless, dolphins have good eyesight, and they can see both under water and in the air. Because they need to breathe air, these animals make frequent contact with the surface and may look out of the water to see what is going on above. Dolphins may use their eyes to spot circling sea

Soft rubber cups are put over the eyes of dolphins in experiments to see how accurate their sonar system is.
MARINELAND OF FLORIDA

This dolphin sees well above water.
DELLA SCHULER
ANDERSON/DOLPHIN
RESEARCH CENTER

birds in the distance that are feeding on schools of fish. We know their eyesight can be quite accurate, since performing dolphins can leap twenty feet from the water and take fish from the hand of the trainer.

The sense of smell is absent in dolphins. They seem to be able to taste, however, since individuals may have favorite foods. Taste could be used to communicate some close-range messages through the water from one dolphin to another, such as readiness to mate, but so far we know little about such signals.

Because they are social animals, the sense of touch must be important to them. They touch often, laying a flipper across another dolphin's back or swimming so close together that their bodies brush. They also nose one another with their beaks.

Touch is important in dolphin social life. DAN FEICHT, CEDAR POINT, SANDUSKY, OHIO

LIVING IN SCHOOLS

"There's safety in numbers" seems to be a rule followed by dolphins, since they are usually found in groups, called schools. Dolphins living out at sea, where sharks are most likely to attack, tend to be found in large groups. Common dolphins may travel in gigantic schools estimated to number in the thousands, while a herd of spotted dolphins can have 1,000 or more animals. In shallow water, dolphin schools are smaller. The bottle-nosed dolphin, which inhabits the coast, has twenty or fewer animals in a school. The harbor porpoise, which stays in shallow water, usually lives in groups of only two to ten individuals. Only some of the river dolphins live alone.

There are other reasons for schooling besides safety. Far out at sea, a lone animal might have trouble finding a mate. On land, many creatures that live alone use scent to attract members of the opposite sex from far away. But scent won't work at distances in the water. By living in groups, dolphins ensure that finding a mate will not be a problem.

Spotted dolphins travel in large schools. © DOTTE LARSEN

The Mystery of Dolphin Feeding

Schooling also helps dolphins find food. These animals feed mainly on squid and fish that live in schools as well. For this reason, either there is little food around or there is enough to feed everyone. Dolphin schools spread out widely as they swim, increasing the likelihood of encountering something to eat.

Just how dolphins manage to capture their prey is puzzling, however. They all have teeth, but some species have only eight; others have as many as 250. These animals have no legs or tentacles for grasping prey, and it is hard to imagine even an agile dolphin snatching enough fast-swimming, healthy fish to feed itself adequately.

Dolphins often cooperate in feeding, encircling the prey fish like a living net. Human observers have sometimes noticed that this makes the trapped fish easy to capture. No one knows for sure why, but the encircled prey often can't swim quickly. One scientist who encountered a school of fish surrounded by Pacific striped dolphins could pick them up at the

Dusky dolphins can herd fish together for easier feeding.
BERND AND MELANY WÜRSIG

surface with his own hands. The fish could have been in a state of shock from panic, or they might have been totally exhausted from being chased long and hard. But an even more interesting idea has been proposed.

Scientists think that some dolphins might use their versatile sound-producing system to confuse or stun their prey. In captivity, fish in dolphin tanks have ended up mysteriously motionless, unable to swim. At least one investigator found out the hard way just how powerful the sound beams of a dolphin can be. D. C. Reed was swimming at a marine park with a bottle-nosed dolphin that seemed upset. The dolphin went into a strange maneuver, doing a rolling front somersault. Suddenly, Reed felt a powerful impact that lifted his body halfway out of the water. A sharp pain hit his ear, along with a whistling sound, breaking his eardrum.

Recently, scientists found that killer whales (which are very big dolphins) emit sounds while hunting at just the same frequency that herring, the whales' favorite food, hear best. By flooding the fish with sound, the whales could make them confused, unable to use their sense of hearing to find their way about.

A similar hunting technique has been proposed for the sperm whale, which feeds in total darkness at the bottom of the sea. Sperm whales don't even get teeth until they are about ten years old, and whales with twisted lower jaws that could hardly be effective in capturing prey seem to be perfectly healthy otherwise. If these animals could all stun their prey and then pick out the helpless fish or squid at leisure, their success in the ocean world would make a lot more sense.

SENDING SOUND

Even though the dolphin's sonar system is crucial to its life, we understand very little about how the sounds are sent or received. These animals lack vocal cords, and how they make sounds is still a mystery. In addition to the rapid clicks used in sonar, dolphins make whistles, which usually last from about a half-second to several seconds. Dolphins also produce bursts of sound made up of clicks. The resulting noises sound to us like yapping, barking, groaning, or yelping. Since dolphins can make clicks and whistles separately or at the same time, the noises must be produced independently.

The air passages in the dolphin's head are very complex, with several different sacs that open into them. Scientists think these sacs and possibly the larynx could be the sources of sounds, but no one knows just how the system works. Sometimes, when a dolphin whistles, air bubbles come out of the blowhole. But the clicking sounds are always made without loss of air from the system.

You can see the blowhole at the top of this cut-open, dead harbor porpoise. Notice that the blowhole leads to other cavities in the head. Somehow, these are involved in the animal's ability to make sounds.
KEN BALCOMB/ORES

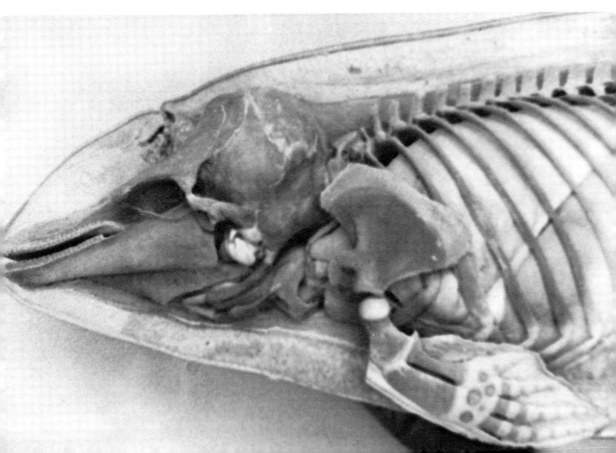

You can see the melon clearly on this bottle-nosed dolphin. U.S. NAVY

On the front of its head, a dolphin has an area called the melon. The melon is filled with oil that is a good transmitter of sound. Some scientists believe that the melon helps to focus sounds as they are sent out from the head of the dolphin, much as a glass lens can focus light. In order for the dolphin to get such detailed information from its sonar, there must be a way to send out the stream of clicks accurately. And if it uses sound to stun its prey, a strongly focused sound would be more powerful than a diffused one. The anatomy of dolphins supports the idea that sounds are produced in the air passages and focused by the melon. The upper front surface of the dolphin skull is concave, or shaped like a dish. In species that live in the open ocean, where the water is clear, the dish is shallow. Dolphins that spend time close to the shore, where the water is more likely to be cloudy, have a deeper depression. Species like the blind river dolphins, which

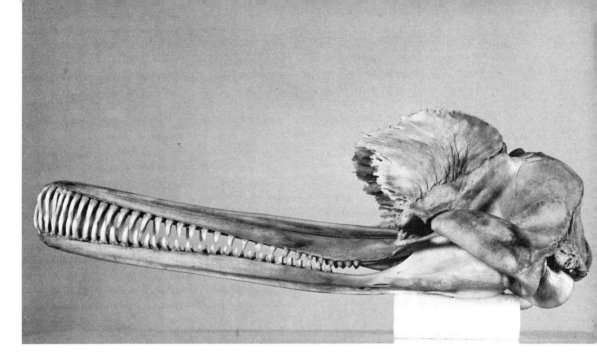

The skull bones of river dolphins, such as the Ganges River dolphin, form a tunnel that is thought to focus the sound beam even more exactly than in dolphins that live in clearer waters. STEINHART AQUARIUM

rely completely on sound for survival, have a tunnel-like extension of the skull bones along the front of the skull. Scientists think that the skull depression reflects the echolocating sound to the melon, which then focuses it into a beam. The oceangoing species would have less need for a narrow beam, because they can see quite well. The blind river dolphins, on the other hand, require a very narrow beam to give them the accuracy necessary to perceive the details of their environment.

SENSING AND USING SOUND

Scientists know little about how dolphins sense sound. The ear has only a tiny opening to the outside. But the narrow canal leading to the middle ear is surrounded by blubber, which conducts low-frequency sounds quite well. Dolphins

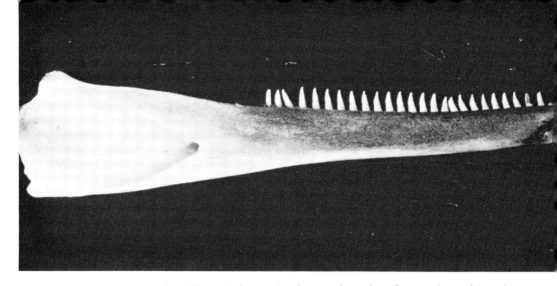

At the back of a dolphin's lower jawbone, there is a depression where the bone is thinner. This area may be involved in hearing sonar echoes.
RANDALL WELLS, DOLPHIN BIOLOGY RESEARCH ASSOCIATION

can perceive very high sounds, with a frequency of 150,000 cycles per second. (Humans can only hear sounds as high as 20,000 cycles per second.) How might these sounds be heard? Sounds appear to reach the middle and inner ears through both the bone and soft tissues around the ear. Another pathway, possibly useful in hearing sonar echoes, is through the sides of the lower jaw. On each side of the lower jaw is a channel of fat similar to that in the melon. A region of the jawbone in the middle of this area is very thin, and the fat channel leads right back to the middle ear. Scientists have shown that this fat channel can carry high-frequency sounds to the ear.

The chains of high-frequency clicks made by dolphins are used in echolocation. But the two other kinds of sounds—the whistles and the variable squawking, groaning clicks—are probably used by dolphins to communicate to one another. In at least some species that whistle, each individual has its own "signature whistle," which other dolphins can recognize. Whistling species tend to travel in very large herds, while nonwhistling kinds live in small groups or alone. Some scientists think the whistles are used for sending other signals besides identifying the individual animals.

The meanings of the clicks are hard to uncover. In the ocean, it is impossible to distinguish which animals are making the sounds as they are recorded, and the behavior of the animals under water is very difficult to observe. Even in captivity, it is hard to tell which dolphin is producing the recorded clicks, since there is no external sign of sound production. Thus, while this expressive chatter does seem to communicate from one dolphin to another, we do not know what messages are being sent.

Dolphin Families

The most important social unit in wild dolphins is the mother and her calf. Almost always, the mother gives birth to just one baby ten to twelve months after mating. Twins are very rare. Dolphins are usually born tail first. Right after birth, the mother may help her baby reach the surface for its first vital breath if it has trouble getting there on its own. The young dolphin must be able to survive at sea from the beginning, and it is born with its eyes, ears, and swimming muscles well developed. It is also very big. Newborn dolphin calves are often almost half as long as their mothers. Like a cow calf, the baby dolphin can move about on its own and take in the world right away, even though it depends on its mother for food and protection.

The mother and calf stay close together. Like other mammals, dolphins feed their babies with mother's milk. The mother's two nipples are tucked away in grooves along the sides of her body midway to the tail flukes. When the baby

A dolphin is born. MARINELAND OF FLORIDA

A North Pacific bottle-nosed dolphin with her baby
SEA LIFE PARK, NICKI CLANCEY

feeds, the nipple pops up and the calf grasps it with its tongue. Milk squirts into the baby's mouth. Dolphin milk is very rich. It is only 40 to 50 percent water (cow's milk is 90 percent water) and 40 to 50 percent fat (cow's milk is less than 4% fat). Baby dolphins grow very quickly and may begin to eat some fish when they are about six months old. While the length of time the young dolphin stays with its mother isn't known for many species, most mothers appear to take care of their young for more than a year and to bear a new calf every two or three years.

STRANDING

Whole groups of dolphins, especially many of the large ones that are popularly called whales, may strand on a beach and seem unable or unwilling to go back into the water. Individual animals may strand like this also; chances are such dol-

A mass stranding of false killer whales COURTESY MIAMI SEAQUARIUM

phins are weak and ill and may be coming into shallow water where it is easier to get to the surface to breathe. The mass strandings of whole herds, however, is a mystery. Sometimes one or more of the animals in such a group suffer from parasites or injuries, but at other times they seem to have no physical illness. Even when people turn the animals back toward the sea and coax them to swim away, they will turn and head again into the beach.

Recently, there are scientists who have suggested that some strandings may be caused by a change in the magnetic field in the region where the dolphins strand. Many animals, such as certain fish and birds, use the magnetic field of the earth to help them navigate during migration. If whales also use a magnetic sense to navigate, such disturbances might confuse the animals into stranding.

KILLING DOLPHINS

In recent years, people have become very concerned about the killing of whales for meat and blubber. The International Whaling Commission regulates the hunting of the large great whales around the world. But no such international organization exists to monitor the killing of small toothed whales and dolphins. Since the Marine Mammal Protection Act was passed in 1972, killing dolphins has been largely outlawed for Americans, although thousands still die accidentally in the nets of tuna fishermen. In some parts of the world, dolphins are hunted for their meat and blubber. In 1985, over 82,000 small toothed whales, including 60,000 dolphins, were killed.

2
Introducing a Few Dolphins

BECAUSE DOLPHINS ARE DIFFICULT TO STUDY, VERY LITTLE IS known about most kinds. A few kinds, however, do well in captivity or live near the shore, where they are easier to watch and collect, so we know more about them. Our information about some species, such as spinners and spotted dolphins, comes mostly from the sad fact that so many are captured by fishermen.

AMAZON RIVER DOLPHIN

The Amazon River dolphin (*Inia geoffrensis*), or boutu, is a member of the small family Platanistidae. All these kinds live in tropical rivers. The Amazon River dolphin inhabits the Orinoco River as well as the Amazon and its tributaries. Its range includes parts of Peru, Venezuela, Ecuador, Colombia, Brazil, Bolivia, and Guyana. It has broad, flexible flippers and wide flukes, which are probably adaptations to slow swimming. Instead of a dorsal fin, it has a low ridge that reaches to the tail. It may reach 9.75 feet (3 meters) in length and can weigh almost 200 pounds (90 kilograms). The ani-

An Amazon River dolphin KEN BALCOMB/ORES

mals vary in color: younger animals are gray on top and pink below, turning gradually paler as they grow older, until the entire body is a pale pink. Though its eyes are small, this dolphin can see as well as utilize its sonar to navigate and find food. It uses its long, thin beak to feed on fish and turtles, grasping the food with the many interlocking teeth in its jaws. Unlike other dolphins, these animals have hairs on their beak. Perhaps they are used to help find food in the muddy bottom of the river.

Boutus live alone or in small groups, often of only three individuals, though as many as twenty may appear together. When swimming, the animals keep their bodies in close contact. Young are born from July to September, between nine and twelve months after the adults mate. Boutus are some times kept in oceanariums, where they spend much of their time lying on the bottom of the tank, turning their heads this way and that, as if watching the people pass by. They also swim upside down; some scientists believe that their sonar works better in this position.

THE SPINNER DOLPHIN

The graceful and sleek spinners (*Stenella longirostris*) are among the most dramatic dolphin acrobats. Their name comes from their habit of jumping up and spinning in the air. Their antics include other spectacular stunts, such as leaping forward out of the water, flinging the tail over the head in a flip, and landing with a loud slap of the tail. Although all spinners belong to the same species, there are obvious differences among different populations. Most spinners are a shade of

A spinner dolphin showing its great acrobatic skills
BERND AND MELANY WÜRSIG

gray above and lighter or white below, but Hawaiian spinners have three colors—dark gray on the back, light gray along the sides, and white underneath. These animals have a small dorsal fin and longer, thinner flippers than spinners from other waters. Male spinners reach about 6.6 feet (2 meters) in length, while females are slightly smaller.

Spinners live in very large groups, sometimes of one thousand or more individuals. They inhabit the Pacific coasts of South and Central America, southern North America, Hawaii, the Indian Ocean, and the tropical portions of the Atlantic.

For a long time, little was known about this common species. Then, in 1963, four spinners were exhibited at Sea Life Park in Hawaii, and knowledge about them began to grow. Unfortunately, however, most of our information about these animals is derived from studies of the countless individuals

Hawaiian spinners, one with a baby SEA LIFE PARK, NICKI CLANCEY

trapped in the nets of tuna fishermen. When the fishermen discovered that spinners and spotted dolphins associated with large schools of yellowfin tuna, they began to use the easily seen dolphins as a clue to where to put out their enormous nets. While the fishermen were in the process of capturing tuna, millions of dolphins were killed. Either they drowned or were injured so badly during capture that they died. Between 1959 and 1972, 4.8 million dolphins, mostly spinners and spotted dolphins, died in tuna nets in the eastern tropical Pacific Ocean.

After the Marine Mammal Protection Act was passed, court battles pitted conservationists against the fishing industry, and fishermen were finally forced to change their methods at the end of 1975. Now a section of finely meshed net called the Medina panel is put at the far end of the net, away from the boat, where the fleeing dolphins used to get tangled in the net and drown. The net may also be relaxed during the gathering so that the top sinks a bit, allowing dolphins to escape over the top. Sometimes people in inflatable rafts enter the nets to help the dolphins get away. Dolphins that have been captured more than once may just lie quietly in the net until they can escape. The limit for U.S. fishermen was set in 1980 at 20,500 animals each year. The federal government puts observers on the tuna boats to keep track of how many dolphins die. The number killed remained below the limit until 1986. In that year, the limit was reached, causing real problems both for tuna fishermen and conservationists.

SPOTTED DOLPHINS

There are two species of spotted dolphin, the pantropical spotted dolphin (*Stenella attenuata*) and the Atlantic spotted

Spotted dolphins RANDALL WELLS, DOLPHIN BIOLOGY RESEARCH ASSOCIATION

dolphin (*Stenella plagiodon*). The pantropical spotted dolphin grows to about 7 feet (2.1 meters) long and weighs up to 280 pounds (127 kilograms). It is one of the fastest dolphins yet clocked and can swim at almost 25 miles (40.2 kilometers) per hour for short sprints. The pantropical spotted dolphin lives in tropical regions of the Pacific Ocean, as far south as Australia and New Zealand, often in association with spinners. Pantropical spotted dolphins are steel gray on top and lighter gray below. Adults have many small gray spots, while young animals lack spots. The young are born eleven months or so after mating and are nursed by their mothers for around a year and eight months. Females can breed at about nine years of age and bear young every two or three years.

More spotted dolphins than spinners have been victims of the tuna fishermen. The association of spotted dolphins, spinners, and yellowfin tuna is somewhat of a mystery. Spinners feed at night and spotted dolphins during the day, so some scientists believe that, by traveling together, one kind of dolphin is alert to danger at all hours. Spotted dolphins feed mainly within 98 feet (30 meters) of the surface, while spin-

A close-up of the spotted skin RANDALL WELLS, DOLPHIN BIOLOGY RESEARCH ASSOCIATION

ners tend to feed at depths of up to 200 feet (61 meters). The tuna feed on the same crabs, squid, and fish that spotted dolphins do and will follow those dolphins rather than the spinners if the group is disrupted.

The Atlantic spotted dolphins look much like their cousins, except that they are blue instead of gray and have a more heavyset body and a thicker beak. They are also a bit larger, reaching 7.5 feet (2.3 meters) in length and 280 pounds (127 kilograms). They are the most spotted of all dolphins. The young are born a lighter color and without spots; they can be confused with bottle-nosed dolphins. While the spotted dolphin rarely rides the bow waves of ships, the Atlantic species frequently travels with ships for long distances. They are quite friendly and may swim close enough for swimmers and divers to touch them. They live usually in groups of fifty or

This fishing net is being let down so the captured dolphins can get away and won't drown. WILLIAM L. HIGH, NOAA

fewer animals, although several hundred are sometimes found together.

THE COMMON DOLPHIN

The common dolphin (*Delphinus delphis*) is the most widely distributed of cetaceans other than the killer whale. It is found in all the world's oceans, except for polar waters. Many people associate this species with the ancient Greek tales of boys riding dolphins and with real-life stories of dolphins volun-

Common dolphins speeding along the water's surface U.S. NAVY

tarily associating with people. When true, however, these accounts more likely deal with the familiar bottle-nosed dolphin. While the bottle-nosed dolphin often comes close to shore, the common dolphin rarely does. Over most of its range, the common dolphin is shy and doesn't do well in close contact with humans. The bottle-nosed dolphin, however, is known to approach people along the shore and adapts very readily to captivity and to human friendship. Out at sea, the common dolphin is a frequent and accomplished bow-wave rider. It may stay with a ship for miles, hoisting its body up onto the wave created by the bow and "surfing" its way along with the ship.

The common dolphin is the most strikingly colored species. Its streamlined, slim body is marked with a variety of hues. The back is black or purplish brown, and the belly is white or cream. The black extends down the sides of the animal in a V just under the dorsal fin, where it meets an upward extension of the white of the belly. The sides in front of the dorsal fin are gray, grayish green, or tan, while the area behind, where the white and black meet, is gray. The crisscross pattern formed by the four colors is very distinctive and beautiful. The beak is usually black and often has a noticeable white tip. The chin is dark, and a stripe connects it to the dark flipper, while another stripe extends from the top of the beak to the eye, where it spreads out in a dark eye patch.

Common dolphins grow to be 7 to 8 feet (2.1 to 2.4 meters) long and weigh from 200 to 300 pounds (91 to 136 kilograms). Males are usually a bit bigger than females. Calves are born in the spring and the fall, ten to eleven months after the

The common dolphin has a lovely crisscross pattern of black, white, and gray along its sides. RANDALL WELLS, UNIVERSITY OF CALIFORNIA-SANTA CRUZ

adults mate, and are nursed for from one to three years. The animals can breed when three or four years old. Many varieties of the common dolphin exist which may be distinct enough to be called separate species. Besides differing in physical characteristics, they may vary in temperament as well. While common dolphins in most of the world are not exhibited in oceanariums because they do not adapt well to captivity, in New Zealand they have been trained to do the same familiar tricks as the adaptable bottle-nosed dolphin and appear to be quite content. A common dolphin named Dipper in New Zealand holds the world's jumping record at 21 feet, 6 inches (6.6 meters).

Huge herds of common dolphins are encountered sometimes extending for more than 30 miles and consisting of a half million or more animals. They are great jumpers, and a herd of common dolphins on the horizon can resemble a stormy sea because of the churning and splashing water. They rest during the day and feed at night. These animals, as well as some other dolphins such as spinners, feed mostly on the organisms that make up the "deep scattering layer." The ocean depths have canyons and mountains, just like the land. Where there are large irregularities under the sea, currents in the water rise up, carrying nutrients and small organisms. These in turn attract fish and other animals such as shrimp and jellyfish, which move up from the depths at night to feed on them. The large groups of hungry animals are called the "deep scattering layer" because they scatter the sound beams of sonar used on ships to measure the depth.

At night, the deep scattering layer drifts upward to within the diving range of dolphins. The dives are usually no more than 150 feet (45.7 meters) and last less than a minute. Common dolphins may also feed on the surface, sometimes leaping from the water to catch a jumping fish in midair.

THE PACIFIC WHITE-SIDED DOLPHIN

This common and very athletic dolphin (*Lagenorhynchus obliquidens*) inhabits the Pacific coasts of North America and Japan. It reaches a length of 7 or 8 feet (2.1 to 2.4 meters) and weighs at least 330 pounds (150 kilograms). Its back and flukes are black. The dorsal fin and flippers are mostly black, with white on the back edges. The sides are gray, with a white area that reaches from the forehead back to the front edge of the flukes. The short beak is black, and the belly is white.

Pacific white-sided dolphins often travel in large herds with

A leaping Pacific white-sided dolphin U.S. NAVY

other species, especially common dolphins and northern right whale dolphins. These schools churn with activity, with much leaping about. The Pacific white-sided dolphin is one of the most active, splashy species of all. It does quite well in captivity, even though it normally lives in deep water, and its breathtaking jumps thrill oceanariuim visitors, especially in California. It has a signature whistle unique to each individual.

In the wild, these animals accompany the migrations of the northern anchovy, a small schooling fish. In the summer and fall, anchovies are found near the shore, where the dolphins follow them to feast. In winter and spring, when the anchovies move farther out, so do the dolphins.

THE HARBOR PORPOISE

The harbor porpoise (*Phocoena phocoena*) is the smallest oceanic cetacean. It usually reaches about 6 feet (1.75 meters) in length and 132 pounds (60 kilograms) in weight. Only the Franciscana (*Pontoporia blainvillei*), which lives in South American rivers, is smaller.

The harbor porpoise has no beak. Its body is chunky. Its back is brown or dark gray, fading to lighter gray along the side and belly. There is a dark stripe leading from the eye to the flipper. Its dorsal fin, flukes, and flippers are all relatively small.

Harbor porpoises probably first breed at three or four years of age. The young are born after eleven months and are thought to nurse for around eight months. They may live to about fifteen years of age.

As its name indicates, the harbor porpoise inhabits shallow water. It doesn't make long dives, usually staying down no

A harbor porpoise calf SUSAN KRUSE, WEST COAST WHALE RESEARCH
FOUNDATION

more than two minutes. It lives along the coasts of the Northern Hemisphere and sometimes swims up rivers as well. A
harbor porpoise may stay in one small area for the summer,
leaving only occasionally. As winter approaches, it will de-
part for more southern waters.

A few harbor porpoises have been seen off the southern
California coast, but it is more common to sight them from
Point Conception northward, all the way into the Gulf of
Alaska. In the East, these animals live as far south as North
Carolina (especially in the winter) and are common in the

Gulf of Saint Lawrence and the Bay of Fundy. The harbor porpoise was once common in European waters but is now quite rare in some areas, such as the Baltic Sea and off the coasts of France. Pollution, oil spills, fishing nets, boat traffic, and other human disturbances are especially hard on a marine animal that lives close to shore.

Even though it commonly lives near human habitation, this porpoise is not often seen, for it doesn't ride bow waves and tends to avoid boats and people in general. Although difficult to capture, the harbor porpoise has been exhibited in oceanariums, but it rarely adapts well to captivity. Some harbor porpoises have been trained to jump through hoops, play ball, and perform other tricks, but even those that are trained rarely live more than two years after capture.

3
The Life of the Bottle-nosed Dolphin

BECAUSE OF ITS POPULARITY IN OCEANARIUM SHOWS AND ON television, the bottle-nosed dolphin is the most familiar to the public. It is also the best known to science. Some scientists identify three species of bottle-nosed dolphins, but they are all quite similar. The Atlantic bottle-nosed dolphin (*Tursiops truncatus*) is the most common performer and the most thoroughly studied. These entertaining animals are about 8 feet (2.4 meters) long and weigh around 400 pounds (181 kilograms). Individuals as long as 13 feet (4 meters) and weighing 1,450 pounds (650 kilograms) have been found. Males tend to be larger than females, and adults are more heavyset than youngsters.

The animals are usually silvery gray, darker above than below. There is quite a bit of color variation, and the color may be browner, bluer, or more purplish gray. Some animals sport a stripe from the eye to the flipper, while others have a ring around the eye. Older animals sometimes are covered with small spots.

The distinct beak of the bottle-nosed dolphin, with the slightly upturned line of the mouth that resembles a human smile, has become a dolphin "trademark" to many people.

Captive bottle-nosed dolphins enjoy
the company of humans.
MARINELAND OF FLORIDA

Each dolphin has seventy-two to a hundred small, sharp teeth. The vertebrae in the neck of most dolphins grow together, so their necks can't move. Five of the seven vertebrae in the neck of the bottle-nosed, however, are unfused, so it can turn its head at an angle to its body. This ability can be exploited by trainers, who can get their charges to shake their heads no and nod their heads yes.

HOW THE BOTTLE-NOSED DOLPHIN LIVES

Bottle-nosed dolphins live along the coasts of practically all the world's seas and oceans except near the poles. Scientists

The natural "smile" of the bottle-nosed dolphin is hard to resist.
DAN FEICHT, CEDAR POINT, SANDUSKY, OHIO

Bottle-nosed dolphins live in schools.
RANDALL WELLS, DOLPHIN BIOLOGY RESEARCH ASSOCIATION

believe that there are actually two types of bottle-nosed dolphin, one that stays close to shore and another that lives offshore and around islands. More is known about the variety that lives close to shore, since it is easier to observe.

Bottle-nosed dolphins often enter bays and lagoons and sometimes even swim up rivers. The coastal type lives in schools of a dozen or so individuals. Some schools seem to consist of a mature male along with several females and their young less than two years old. Other schools are made up of males and/or females that haven't yet reached maturity. Adult males may also live together in schools. Within each school, new animals join and others leave quite frequently, more so than with land mammals that live in similar small groups. The offshore type appears to live in schools of about twenty-five animals. These groups may combine to form large herds of several hundred individuals.

Bottle-nosed dolphins cooperate in chasing fish. Scientists have watched these dolphins herding fish—sometimes toward shore, where they can easily capture them in the shallow water, and sometimes up to the surface of the water, where they can catch the leaping fish in midair. The dolphins may also surround their prey. One large group of about two hundred dolphins was watched as the animals sped, spreading out in a straight line, behind a school of fish. A few of the dolphins then raced ahead and turned back into the mass of fish, forcing them against the dolphins behind. Thus surrounded, the fish could not easily escape, and the dolphins feasted.

Dolphins also learn that fishermen throw unwanted kinds of fish overboard, and they will follow the boats to gather them. In some cases they have even learned to drive fish into the waiting nets of fishermen. The net provides the barrier that makes the fish easier for the dolphins to catch, and the fishermen can gather up the fish that the dolphins don't eat. The offshore bottle-nosed dolphins like squid and are often found associated with another squid-eating cetacean, the pilot whale.

Bottle-nosed dolphins have excellent eyesight out of water. It may seem strange that a completely aquatic animal should have such good eyesight in air, but there are times, like when they feed on jumping fish, that their vision in air is of critical importance. Dolphins may even leave the water completely to feed. In Georgia, one scientist watched while dolphins drove fish onto a mudbank and slid all but their tail flukes out of the water and onto the mud to eat the fish.

These graceful animals need only to expose their blowholes at the surface to breathe, but when they are swimming along, they often leap up in the air for no apparent reason. Sometimes this is done during the rapid pursuit of fish schools. Other dolphin species "fly" through the air while chasing down fish as well. This habit has been given the name "porpoising."

Coastal bottle-nosed dolphins are generally homebodies, usually tending to stay in the same area or, if they do wander

Bottle-nosed dolphins
can see well in air.
SEA LIFE PARK,
NICKI CLANCEY

A bottle-nosed
dolphin, jumping.
RANDALL WELLS,
UNIVERSITY OF CALIFORNIA–SANTA CRUZ

Carolina Snowball, an albino dolphin COURTESY MIAMI SEAQUARIUM

about, returning soon to a familiar home range. Sometimes they have two different home areas. A pure white albino named Carolina Snowball became very familiar to fishermen along the South Carolina coast in the early 1960s. After being seen often in this very limited area, she would disappear for weeks at a time. Meanwhile, an albino dolphin would appear off the Georgia coast and stay for some weeks. Then she would vanish. Although the observations were not checked for exact times to be sure this was the same dolphin, when Carolina Snowball was captured and taken to the Miami Seaquarium, the Georgia albino disappeared for good as well. More careful studies by scientists have also indicated that bottle-nosed dolphins do have such familiar home areas.

SOCIAL LIFE

Most of what we know about this animal comes from studying individuals in captivity. As already discussed, this dolphin quickly adapts to the presence of humans and is very relaxed around them. It is also friendly to other dolphins, even those of other species. Several oceanariums now have breeding colonies of bottle-nosed dolphins, and they have bred for at least five generations away from their natural environment.

This animal is so successful in captivity for several reasons. It is adapted to life in shallow water and tends not to wander over vast areas in the wild, so perhaps it doesn't feel too confined in a large concrete tank. Because it lives close to shore, it is used to having barriers around it, so its sonar doesn't become easily confused by the echoes from the walls of the tank. Social life is very important to these animals, and several of them are usually kept together in the same tank so that they can develop normal social relationships.

The most important family tie for dolphins is between the mother and her calf. Baby bottle-nosed dolphins are born at different times of year, depending on where the animals live. Off the Florida coast, February through May is the usual season for births. The baby grows in its mother's body for a year. When it is born, it is from 3.3 to 4.1 feet (1 to 1.25 meters) long and weighs from 20 to 26.5 pounds (9 to 12 kilograms). It nurses for a year to eighteen months, although it may start eating a few fish when it is six months old. Females are ready to reproduce as early as five years after birth and have a baby every two or three years. Males may breed at the age of nine. In captivity, a bottle-nosed dolphin can live to be twenty-five to thirty-five years old.

Mother and baby bottle-nosed dolphins MARINELAND OF FLORIDA

While the young dolphins rely on their mothers for food and protection, they are quite curious and may wander off to explore. If danger threatens, the mother may have to search for her baby, who sometimes interprets her pursuit as a chasing game rather than something serious. In captivity, frustrated mothers have been seen to pin an especially energetic baby onto the floor of the tank in an apparent effort to get it to stay close to her rather than to be too adventuresome. After such a treatment, which the little one endures with much vocal protest, it stays with her for some hours.

In addition to its mother, the baby may have a protector nicknamed the "auntie," another adult female that doesn't have a baby of her own. The auntie helps watch over the baby, and the two of them may swim off together without protest from the mother. In captivity, dolphins of different species may serve as aunties to one another.

Dolphin Play

Wild bottle-nosed dolphins play in the surf, riding the waves in to shore much like human surfers. They may surf for an hour in the same place, catching the waves as they roll in, and slipping away at the last moment before the waves crash on the beach. They may also harass whales into making waves

Bottle-nosed dolphins at play MARINELAND OF FLORIDA

for them. Scientists watching bottle-nosed dolphins off the coast of Argentina saw them travel out of their way to get near migrating southern right whales. The dolphins would swim back and forth across the whales' heads until the whales snorted and lunged at the dolphins. The surging forward of these huge animals created pressure waves, which the dolphins then rode, much as they do with the bow waves of ships. In Hawaii, it is quite common to see bottle-nosed dolphins ride the bow waves of the humpback whales that visit the islands each winter.

In marshy areas, bottle-nosed dolphins may play in the mud, getting up a good head of steam and then sliding out of the water onto the wet, slippery banks. This behavior may be repeated over and over again and is not associated with feeding or any other "practical" activity.

Like puppies and kittens, young dolphins like to play with each other. They play chasing games and sometimes convince adults to join in. They also play keep-away with objects such as dead fish or things that somehow get into the tank. Although it is difficult to observe dolphin behavior in the wild, playing by young animals has been seen. Two scientists once watched four immature bottle-nosed dolphins leaping over the bodies of adults in the school and chasing one another. They saw single animals tossing around bits of seaweed and fish skin and even chasing butterflies by jumping out of the water.

COMMUNICATING

With bottle-nosed dolphins, we have some idea of the functions of the sounds they make. The unique whistle made by each individual can easily be recognized both by humans and by other dolphins. One animal was tested to see just how accurately he could distinguish the whistles of other bottle-nosed dolphins. A tape of the whistles of eight individuals, recorded at different times under varying circumstances, was played to him. He could pick out the whistle of any one dolphin without making a mistake. Eight months later, he could still do it perfectly. Clearly, bottle-nosed dolphins can recognize one another easily by their whistles. Now and then an individual comes along that does not have such a consistent whistle. The sounds of such animals are more difficult to identify, both by dolphins and people.

While each whistle is unique enough to function like a signature for the dolphin, it is still varied in ways that communicate other information. The pitch and loudness can vary with the emotional state of the animal. In panic, for example,

The dolphin TV star Flipper performs with other dolphins at the Miami Seaquarium. COURTESY MIAMI SEAQUARIUM

the whistle is louder and higher-sounding. Under some circumstances, the whistle can be the merest chirp, while at other times it may be a long, uninterrupted blast. A mother and calf that have been separated may whistle repeatedly for each other, while a frightened animal may quiet down and hardly whistle so as to remain inconspicuous. A very alarmed animal, such as one removed from the water for some reason, may emit a "whistle-squawk"—the signature whistle combined with a series of pulsed clicks.

Pulses of clicks are also used to communicate other information. In some cases, specific sounds are associated with particular behavior. For example, a bottle-nosed dolphin may react to sudden danger with a sharp, cracking sound. Other dolphins would understand this as a warning. But there is more to this animal's language than such predictable noises. Most of their sounds can't be so neatly described, since they vary depending on the emotional state of the animal.

In addition to sounds made by their "voices," bottle-nosed dolphins have other ways of communicating. When one dolphin threatens another, it snaps its jaws together suddenly, producing a sharp cracking sound. When danger threatens in the wild, a dolphin may slap its tail hard on top of the water, making a loud noise that warns nearby animals. In captivity, this same action is used to show displeasure with a trainer, alarm at new objects in the tank, or frustration.

4
Captive Dolphins

DOLPHINS ARE VERY POPULAR PUBLIC ATTRACTIONS. HUNDREDS of bottle-nosed dolphins, mostly captured off the Florida and Mississippi coasts, perform in oceanariums around the world, as well as a few members of other species such as Pacific white-sided dolphins. A number of killer whales, which are actually very large dolphins, also thrill spectators with their memorable acts.

TRAINING DOLPHINS

Dolphin training has become both a well-developed art and a science. The point of training is to get an animal to perform whenever it is given cues by a human trainer or by a recording. Fortunately, these creatures show every sign of enjoying showing off for people. This willingness makes training them an exciting and rewarding job.

At the very beginning, a dolphin must learn that it will be rewarded, usually with a fish, if it carries out a certain behavior. It also needs to associate the behavior with some sort of cue. Since hearing is the dolphin's most developed sense,

Bottle-nosed dolphins
delight crowds at Marine
World-Africa U.S.A.
DARRYL W. BUSH/MARINE
WORLD-AFRICA U.S.A.

58

a sound cue is generally used, at least at the beginning. Once a dolphin learns the principle of training—that it will get rewards (also called "reinforcement") for performing certain "tricks"—training for a new routine can go very quickly. Sometimes, however, the animal's fear must be overcome before it will perform.

At Hawaii's Sea Life Park, trainer Karen Pryor was putting together the first show, using a pair of spotted dolphins. One act required the dolphins to jump over bars above the water. As a first step in training, Ms. Pryor placed a rope down the side of the tank, across the bottom, and up the

A dolphin receives a fish reward for performing well. DAN FEICHT, CEDAR POINT, SANDUSKY, OHIO

other side. She planned to reward the dolphins every time they crossed the rope and then raise it until it reached the final height above water. Immediately came a snag—the animals were terrified of the rope. They huddled at one end of the tank and refused to get near it, much less swim over it. Nothing would persuade them—neither a ball tossed on the other side nor a fish that was offered there. Finally, in frustration, Ms. Pryor threw a beach chair into the water near the animals. That scared them into zipping across the rope to the other side. As they did so, she blew her whistle and then gave them some fish. A second time she threw in the chair, the dolphins crossed the rope, and she whistled and gave them fish. The third time, they zipped over when they saw her lift the chair.

By then the animals had learned that the rope wouldn't hurt them, and soon they were crossing on purpose, grabbing a fish, and dashing across again for another fish. The next step was to get them to swim over more than once for a fish. When they crossed and didn't hear the whistle, they were puzzled. They tried again and got the whistle and fish. Very quickly, they learned that they wouldn't get a fish every time they swam over the rope. At this point in training, it is important to "randomize" the rewards—not every correct performance is rewarded, and the performer never knows for sure when it will get a payoff. Sometimes the dolphins had to cross four times before hearing the whistle and getting a fish; at other times, they got results by crossing once. Random rewards keep up the excitement of the game, in much the same way that a person keeps trying a slot machine. The hope of a reward is always there, but just when it might come is not certain. This also makes modifying the rewarded behavior easier, since the animal doesn't expect a fish every time. If the trainer wanted to get both animals to swim together over the rope, for example, they would give up soon if they were used to getting a reward every time and suddenly got none. With random reinforcement, however, they will keep trying and probably cross together by accident at first. Then they can learn that they should always cross together.

The next step was raising the rope to the halfway level. If the animals swam under or started to go over and then turned away, they got nothing. They were rewarded only for swimming over it. Once they did that without error, the rope was raised to the surface, and soon they were jumping over it. Adding a metal bar under the rope was easy. By using reinforcement for the correct behaviors in single steps, the trainer was able to get the two dolphins to jump together over the bar, always in the same direction, in just a few training sessions.

Raising the bar above the water caused a new problem: the dolphins refused completely to jump. They were used to locating the bar both by sonar and by sight underwater, and now it was up in the air, where they couldn't locate it. The solution was to put the bar just above the surface, where little waves would splash against it when the dolphins swam about; then they could see it. The animals began to jump again, sloppily at first. Now they were rewarded just for jumping, never mind how nicely. After the dolphins mastered jumping the bar out of the water, the trainer added all the other things they learned earlier until the jumping trick was done right. Then the bar was gradually raised until the dolphins were leaping way out of the water. Using methods like these, trainers can get dolphins to perform an amazing variety of tricks.

Training dolphins to jump over a rope may take patience, but the result is worth the work. DARRYL W. BUSH/MARINE WORLD-AFRICA U.S.A.

DOLPHINS AND PEOPLE

Most individuals act as if they look forward to their learning sessions. If a trainer wants to let a dolphin know that it is not doing its best, he or she can punish the animal simply by turning and walking away from the tank. The dolphin seems to enjoy the training session and doesn't want it to end, so it will then try harder.

Captive dolphins may develop a real attachment to their trainers, sometimes to the point where they won't perform for anyone else. One dolphin at Marineland of Florida was shipped to Sea-Arama Marineworld in Galveston, Texas, after being carefully trained by Fred Lyons. It refused to per-

Dolphins and their
trainers enjoy working
together and can
become very fond of
one another. DAN
FEICHT, CEDAR POINT,
SANDUSKY, OHIO

form at its new home. Some weeks later, Mr. Lyons visited Sea-Arama for other reasons. When he heard about the problem, he examined the dolphin carefully but could find no sign of illness. Then he went through the dolphin's routine with it, and it performed flawlessly, even though there had been no training sessions for weeks. Since the animal was no use in Texas, it was sent back to Florida, where it got to work again with Fred Lyons. While most dolphins are not so particular, often they will be at their best when doing a show with their first trainer.

Captive dolphins also seem to enjoy interacting with humans outside of training and performing. Their playfulness can be a problem for their keepers. While dolphins are at home in the water, they learn quickly that humans on land want to stay dry. Sometimes a dolphin will lie innocently near the water's surface until a passing person turns his back. Suddenly, the animal will come to life, and the human will be soaked by a well-aimed squirt of water.

One especially playful young bottle-nosed dolphin at Marineland of Florida used to offer a ball to any passing person, much as a golden or Labrador retriever will do on land. Like a dog, the dolphin never seemed to tire of the game—the human would always be the one to quit first. This same animal once pulled a trick on a night watchman. The watchman could not see the dolphin in the water as he passed the tank, so he reached over and aimed the beam of his flashlight into the water. The dolphin suddenly appeared and grabbed the flashlight from his hand. This was the beginning of a game of keep-away, with the dolphin in charge. Whenever the watchman almost got a net around the flashlight, the dolphin pushed it farther away. By the time it was finally

A playful dolphin splashes water at the trainer's dog.
SEA LIFE PARK, NICKI CLANCEY

fished out, the flashlight was soaked through and through and completely ruined.

The communication between captive dolphins and their human friends goes both ways. The trainer may work at letting the dolphin know what behavior is wanted, but the dolphin can also tell the trainer a thing or two. If a dolphin in training gets frustrated—such as when a trainer is asking it to do too much too fast—the trainer will find out in short order. The animal may slap its tail hard on the water's surface so that the resulting splash drenches its human co-worker. A wise teacher then slows things down.

When a dolphin wants to play, it has to teach its human friends the rules of the game. If the person is too slow to understand, the dolphin may use the tail-slapping stunt, or it may make loud complaining noises. If it gets really impatient, it may even hit the person with its beak. But once the human friend finally figures out the right way to play, the dolphin can keep up the game for hours on end.

Sometimes routines used in shows are the invention of the dolphins themselves. At Marineland of New Zealand, a common dolphin named Brenda invented a baseball game. One day, trainer Frank Robson stopped to visit with the dolphins while carrying a baseball bat. Brenda swam off, picked up a ball, and stationed herself a few feet from the trainer. He

Brenda, the inventive New Zealand dolphin, plays with a rubber ring.
FRANK D. ROBSON

lifted the bat into position, and Brenda pitched at the bat. Mr. Robson was amazed, for normally dolphins throw a ball directly to a person. When Mr. Robson hit the ball, Brenda dashed off to retrieve it and returned to her pitching position. Mr. Robson called out a strike, and Brenda pitched the ball again. And so began a new dolphin stunt that eventually included Brenda as pitcher and three other dolphins as outfielders, whose job it was to throw the hit ball back to Brenda before Mr. Robson could run to base and back to home.

ENDLESS CURIOSITY

Though dolphins may sometimes be easily frightened by new objects, they are curious animals and can become very involved with activities outside their tanks. One young male bottle-nosed dolphin living alone was given a TV set for entertainment. He could watch the programs either through a window in the side of the tank or by lifting his head out of the water. The dolphin watched television often and preferred lots of action—commercials and variety shows rather than long dramas. One evening, right after the program changed, the dolphin began swimming wildly about, making excited sounds and tossing his ball up in the air, over and over again. His concerned attendants hurried over, worried that something was wrong, only to discover that a baseball game was on the screen! We can't know what the dolphin was thinking, but his behavior was the same as when previously he had offered to play ball and his human partner had refused. The men on television were throwing the ball back and forth to one another, but no one was throwing a ball to the dolphin, and he probably wanted to play, too.

At Marineland of Florida, a female long-finned pilot whale

liked to watch the performing bottle-nosed dolphins in the tank next door. She would rest her head on the edge of her tank and watch her aquatic neighbors. Each day she got more and more involved and kept pulling herself farther and farther out of the water so she could get a better view. One day she climbed too far up and toppled over, landing completely out of the water outside her tank. Attendants quickly checked her and found that, fortunately, she wasn't hurt. They put her back in the water and installed a guard railing so that she couldn't fall out again.

Dolphins can learn a lot by watching. Swifty, a false killer whale at Marineland of Florida, learned an entire dolphin

Pilot whales can also be trained to be star performers.
MARINELAND OF FLORIDA

performance when put in a tank with the trained dolphins, without any training or rewards. At Sea Life Park, two dolphins that had totally different routines once got mixed up by attendants. The trainer didn't recognize the switch and wondered why the first animal was so nervous. She performed all the right stunts, but out of order and quite frantically. When it came time for a jump through a hoop twelve feet above the water, the dolphin jumped sloppily and missed. Rather than criticize the animal, as she would normally do, the concerned trainer lowered the hoop to six feet, and the dolphin leaped through it in a rush.

The second animal's performance involved being blindfolded and passing through a maze of underwater pipes as well as retrieving plastic rings, all using sonar. After the trainer had some trouble putting on the blindfolds, the dolphin rather shakily got through the performance with few errors. Neither animal had been trained in the routine it performed, but both managed to accomplish all the other

A blindfolded dolphin demonstrating its sonar abilities SEA LIFE PARK

animal's stunts. Getting a dolphin to jump through a hoop out of the water usually requires weeks of training. And while the second dolphin had been trained to accept a blindfold, she had never attempted the maze before. Only after the show was over did the trainer discover the error. How many humans performing in a play could unexpectedly take over another person's part so well if suddenly thrust into the spotlight?

Capturing Dolphins

It's true that people get great pleasure from dolphin performances and learn a great deal from captive animals. Yet we must ask ourselves whether it is right to bring wild and free animals into captivity for the entertainment of humans. Because dolphins are such intelligent animals, some people object particularly to depriving them of their freedom. But the question should really be applied to all wild things, not just those we can most easily identify with.

In the United States today, it is only permissible to capture these animals under a special permit, and then only for purposes of exhibition and research. Humane methods of capture and careful tending of the animals during transport result in minimal discomfort for them. Most dolphins lose their fear and become attached to humans quite quickly afterward, and they often have long and productive lives in captivity. Nowadays, more and more dolphins are breeding successfully in oceanariums, so that fewer are caught from the wild. When a concrete tank is all an animal has ever known, some people have less concern that the quality of its life is diminished.

There are problems, however. One might ask about the effect on the wild dolphins when a member of their commu-

Bottle-nosed dolphins breed successfully at many oceanariums, including Marineland of Florida, the first to keep these animals in captivity for a long period of time. MARINELAND OF FLORIDA

nity is lost. And the plain, downright boring environment of a concrete pool can be a prison to an active, curious, and intelligent animal. Many people worry especially about the morality of taking killer whales from the wild and keeping them captive. Bottle-nosed dolphins are relatively small animals, and they can be kept in the same numbers in captivity as would associate with one another in nature. Not so with killer whales. They are so big that most end up living alone in a very confined environment; in the wild they live in groups of up to thirty animals. Killer whales may live to be well over fifty years old. But in captivity, they often die after only a few years. Although the tanks they live in are large by human standards, they are tiny for the whales. And the concrete walls must be very confusing to their sonar, constantly reflecting back any sounds they make.

Captive dolphins, including killer whales, however, have contributed enormously to our knowledge about them and have increased human awareness of the needs of wild things around the world. Perhaps the urgency for understanding in order to save these animals in an increasingly difficult world outweighs the pain and suffering of the individual animals involved.

Some whale lovers question whether killer whales like these should be kept in captivity. DARRYL W. BUSH/MARINE WORLD-AFRICA U.S.A.

5

How "Human" Are Dolphins?

SCIENTISTS HAVE TRADITIONALLY DONE THEIR BEST TO KEEP their distance from the animals they study. They are constantly on the alert to avoid being "anthropomorphic"—attributing human characteristics to their subjects. With some animals, like caterpillars or worms, maintaining a distance from the animals is easy. But with creatures like dolphins, which so clearly exhibit humanlike traits such as caring for one another and intelligence, and even a sense of humor, it becomes just about impossible. Many scientists have reached the point where they are examining the whole idea of animal awareness: Do some animals have feelings like ours? Are some animals able to behave in ways that bring on such feelings, like playing just for the joy of it? And can creatures such as dolphins communicate more than just certain basic messages like the warning of danger?

CARING FOR EACH OTHER

Both in captivity and in the wild, dolphins and whales often show caring behavior toward their own kind. This used to

Because dolphins are so quick to learn, they are believed to be among the most intelligent animals on Earth. DARRYL W. BUSH/MARINE WORLD-AFRICA U.S.A.

lead to disaster for whales that came to the aid of a harpooned animal and ended up dead as well. The most frequently seen caring behavior is called "standing by": when one individual is injured, the others remain nearby rather than swimming off to safety. Sometimes cetaceans get very excited about an injury to another and will swim about frantically, bite harpoon lines, or even charge a ship. Pacific white-sided dolphins often show such behavior. In one instance, an adult female kept swimming between a wounded dolphin and the ship that had harpooned it, trying to shove the injured animal away from the ship. When a cetacean is injured, one or more others will sometimes push under it, helping it reach the surface so that it can breathe.

In captivity, dolphins may even help other species. At Marineland of the Pacific, two Pacific white-sided dolphins helped an injured Dall's porpoise by putting their beaks under its fins and lifting it to the surface where it could breathe. One male spotted dolphin at Sea Life Park consistently helped newly captured animals adjust to the unfamiliar circum-

When a bottle-nosed dolphin calf is born, another animal often stays with the new mother to provide help if needed. MARINELAND OF FLORIDA

stances. He would head them off if they were about to bump into a wall and would even pass them fish to eat.

Captive cetaceans can become very attached to one another. If separated for months, such friends clearly recognize each other and act excited when put together again. The two spotted dolphins at Sea Life Park in Hawaii did everything together. When they swam, they moved as one, overlapping their fins and pressing them together, even as they turned or rose to breathe. The male would put himself between his mate and possible danger, and he would always let her eat first.

Like helpful behavior, friendship can cross species lines. A killer whale and a bottle-nosed dolphin at Sea Life Park that were kept in adjacent tanks figured out how to get together. During the night, the dolphin would leap the barrier separating them, and in the morning, the two friends would be found together. This behavior was a nuisance, because the animals performed at different times, and separating them wasn't easy. To keep the animals apart, the staff added a

This killer whale and white-sided dolphin share a tank at the Miami Seaquarium.
COURTESY MIAMI SEAQUARIUM

heavy board that made the barrier wider and higher so that the dolphin could no longer jump over it. Then the whale took charge and, again at night while it couldn't be observed, used its great strength to knock the barrier down so that its friend could jump over again.

Thinking Ahead

We've already seen that dolphins can learn a great deal from watching one another and that they have a lot of natural curiosity. Such passive learning is not unusual and seems to indicate that the animals think about what they see and remember the details, both of which are aspects of true intelligence. Another example of such learning comes from an oceanarium where one dolphin in a group was trained to raise a flag by jumping from the water to grab a ball attached to the flag and pulling it through the water. Eventually, this animal was taken away and another was trained to raise the flag by bumping the ball with its snout. When this animal died, another immediately substituted, striking the ball without being trained to do so. This animal then refused to perform for a couple of days, and a young animal took over the trick on its own by grabbing the ball and pulling on it to raise the flag, just as the first animal had been taught to do.

Dolphins also show their ability to imitate by copying the behavior of those around them, even of other species. One captive dolphin entertained itself by imitating a seal it lived with. It began to act like a seal, performing such undolphinlike behavior as lying on one side at the surface, flippers outstretched, with flukes out of the water, or scratching its belly with its flippers. This same animal also copied the movements of penguins, turtles, and other animals, and rubbed a feather held in its beak against the walls of its tank in imitation of a human diver cleaning off algae. While doing its diver act, the dolphin blew bubbles and made sounds like those of the human's breathing apparatus. A different dolphin used a bit of tile to scrape seaweed from the bottom of its tank, in imitation of a diver with a vacuum hose; then another dolphin began to copy the dolphin's scraping behavior.

WHAT IS INTELLIGENCE?

In order to come to conclusions about the intelligence of any living being, including a person, some definition of intelligence itself must be made. This is much more difficult than it first appears. While we can recognize "intelligent" behavior sometimes, we may not be able to pin down just what it is that seems so smart. Psychologists and philosophers have wrestled with this problem for generations and not found an answer that everyone would agree with. IQ tests have traditionally included items requiring mathematical skill, reasoning power, and memory. However, a written IQ test requires good reading skills, and a person can be very intelligent but unable to read well. And many people believe that other abilities, such as creativity, are at least as important as mathematical skill. But how do you measure creativity? Some recent tests for humans try to deal with these problems by measuring a large number of components of intelligence rather than just a few.

If we can't agree on what makes a human intelligent, how can we judge the intelligence of animals? Each species alive today exists because it is able to function well within its own environment, to behave in ways that promote its survival and its ability to reproduce. In a sense, every kind of animal is

At the Vancouver Aquarium, bored killer whales discovered that they could tame seagulls to take bits of fish from their mouths. The adult whales were the first to feed the gulls. Now young whales, like those in this photo, also entertain themselves by feeding gulls. Such inventive behavior is considered by many to be a sign of intelligence. PETER THOMAS

smartest at living in its own particular setting. But since we are human, we look at the question differently and want to judge animals by human standards. Thus, we consider problem solving, learning, and communication skills as primary measures of intelligence. Flexibility, which has allowed humans to adapt to every habitat on the face of the earth, is thought of as a crucial aspect of truly intelligent behavior.

Looked at in this way, we can see why people so quickly see cetaceans as intelligent animals. They are curious and can solve problems that face them. They learn very quickly, re-

A trainer gives a hand signal to a dolphin. DARRYL W. BUSH/MARINE WORLD-AFRICA U.S.A.

spond to human communication with them very easily, and appear to communicate among themselves as well. Add to this array the other humanlike traits of caring for one another and playful and mischievous behavior, and it is no wonder that humans identify these fascinating animals as "intelligent."

How Smart Are Dolphins?

Unfortunately, a great deal of publicity has accompanied the claims of some people who have studied dolphins, such as John C. Lilly, who are expressing their opinions and inner feelings rather than the results of carefully conducted experiments. Dr. Lilly believes that dolphins communicate with one another at the same level of sophistication as people, and that we can learn their language and talk with them. However, we know almost nothing about the meanings of the sounds dolphins make and whether those sounds carry complex and variable meanings as do our words, so we are in no position yet to evaluate the complexity of cetacean communication.

Many animals communicate with sound, but communication is not the same as speech. Dogs, for example, understand the meanings of growls, whimpers, and barks. That does not mean that they can talk. Dogs all over the world understand the same sound signals; that understanding is part of their inheritance. Human language, on the other hand, is learned, and varies from one community to another. Each human language has words with specific meanings and a structure that relates the words to one another. In English, for example, the order of words in a sentence determines the meaning. "The man hit the dog" means that the man carried out an action against the dog. In some other languages, endings would be added onto the words for "man" and "dog" to indicate which one performed the action and which received it. In such languages, the word order doesn't matter; the endings tell the story, and the sentence can be worded either way.

Louis M. Herman of the University of Hawaii decided to use a different approach to evaluate the language abilities of dolphins. Dr. Herman designed experiments to see if dolphins had the mental capacity to comprehend artificial languages invented by humans. If they weren't capable of language comprehension, it would indicate that dolphins probably do not have advanced language ability.

Dr. Herman used two bottle-nosed dolphins in his study. Phoenix was trained using a language in which computerized underwater sounds acted as "words" to represent actions and objects. Akeakamai was taught a language in which arm gestures served as words. Each language had a different structure as well. By using two different senses—hearing and sight—and by providing a different grammar for each language, Herman could learn something about how flexible

Trainer Beth Roden signs to Akeakamai "WATER OVER." Notice that Ake is already swimming away while watching to see the final gesture. PHOTO BY LOUIS M. HERMAN, COURTESY OF KEWALO BASIN MARINE MAMMAL LABORATORY.

dolphin language ability is and whether or not it is tied to a particular sense.

Phoenix and Akeakamai both learned their languages thoroughly and, in the process, showed many signs of true language understanding. They easily understood that the word for ball, for example, applied to any ball thrown into the tank, not just to the first ball they saw. They understood the grammar of their languages and acted correctly on commands when familiar words were combined in new ways for the first time. Akeakami could extract the essence of the gestures in her language, since she could understand a variety of human "speakers," whose presentation of the gestures varied considerably. If told to "fetch the ball" when no ball was in the tank, each animal would carry out the command once the ball (along with other objects) was added. Both also learned to report back to the trainer if an object mentioned in a command was not in the tank. They could figure out how to solve problems associated with carrying out commands, too. For example, after learning the names for several objects including "hoop" and the word for "thru" (meaning to swim through an object), Phoenix was taught the concepts of "surface" (for a floating object) and "bottom" (for something lying on the bottom). When first given the command to swim through the bottom hoop, Phoenix ignored the hoop on the surface and headed down. She found the bottom hoop lying flat. She stuck her beak under one edge of the hoop and lifted it until it was almost vertical; then she swam through it. Finally, the dolphins could understand how the order of the words affected the meaning of the command. For example, when Akeakamai was instructed "PIPE HOOP FETCH," she correctly took a floating hoop to a floating pipe. When given "HOOP PIPE FETCH" instead, she correctly brought the pipe to the hoop.

Phoenix has been given the sentence "BOTTOM HOOP THRU." She uses her beak to lift one edge, then swims through. PHOTOS BY ALAN LEVENSON, COURTESY OF KEWALO BASIN MARINE MAMMAL LABORATORY.

Dr. Herman's work shows that dolphins do have the mental capacity to understand the important features of true language. This is a real breakthrough in the study of animal communication. No other creature, including apes, has been shown to have this ability. (Experiments with apes learning language have dealt largely with getting them to produce language rather than understand it. There are serious problems with interpreting the results of this work.) Of course, we still don't know if dolphins are capable of using language actively themselves, as opposed to understanding language presented to them.

The Dolphin Brain

Some dolphins and whales have brains as big in proportion to their body size as do humans. Not only are the dolphin brains large, but they look similar in some ways to ours. The cerebral cortex of the brain is where the thinking takes place, and most animals lack the complex folds that increase the surface area of this part of the human brain. Dolphins, however,

The dolphin brain is large and complex. ALISA SCHULMAN

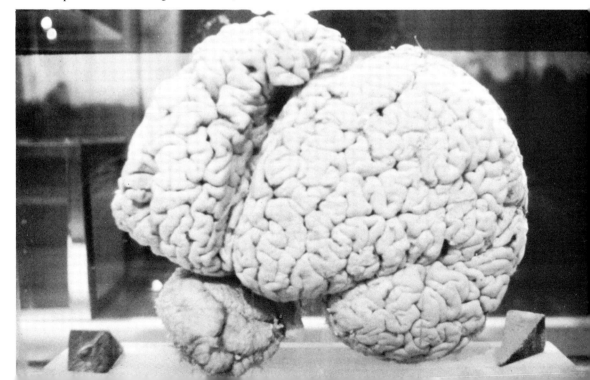

have a very well-developed cerebral cortex, about the same size proportionally as that of humans and apes. The dolphin's brain is much bigger than needed to perform basic functions, even taking the dolphin's remarkable echolocation system into account.

But there are important differences as well. The human cerebral cortex is divided up into many specialized areas, each with a different function. The dolphin cortex, however, is much more uniform in structure. In this way, it is more like the brain of a primitive mammal instead of an advanced one. Thus, the intelligence of these animals seems to be achieved through the sheer size of the brain, through great numbers of similar units, rather like a very big but simply organized computer. When a dolphin behaves "intelligently," it may be doing so by very different brain activity than when a chimpanzee does something that seems "smart."

The discovery that there are such basic differences in the brains of dolphins compared with those of people only makes the obvious communication between these two creatures— one bound to the land, the other wedded to the sea, one tied largely to what its eyes can see, the other to what its ears can hear—all the more amazing and wonderful.

Tuffy, a bottle-nosed dolphin, worked closely with Navy divers during the 1960s. U.S. NAVY

Cetaceans Mentioned in This Book

ODONTOCETI—TOOTHED WHALES

Family *Platanistidae*

Amazon River dolphin	*Inia geoffrensis*
Ganges River dolphin	*Platanista gangetica*
Franciscana	*Pontoporia blainvillei*

Family *Delphinidae*

False killer whale	*Pseudorca crassidens*
Killer whale	*Orcinus orca*
Long-finned pilot whale	*Globicephala melaena*
Atlantic spotted dolphin	*Stenella plagiodon*
Pan-tropical spotted dolphin	*Stenella attenuata*
Spinner dolphin	*Stenella longirostris*
Striped dolphin	*Stenella coeruleoalba*
Dusky dolphin	*Lagenorhynchus obscurus*
Pacific white-sided dolphin	*Lagenorhynchus obliquidens*
Common dolphin	*Delphinus delphis*
Bottle-nosed dolphin	*Tursiops truncatus*
North Pacific bottle-nosed dolphin (considered a separate species, *Tursiops gilli*, by some)	
Risso's dolphin	*Grampus griseus*
Irrawaddy dolphin	*Orcaella brevirostris*

PORPOISES (put into Family *Phocoenidae* by some)

Spectacled porpoise	*Phocoena dioptrica*
Harbor porpoise	*Phocoena phocoena*
Dall's porpoise	*Phocoenoides dalli*

Index

J 599.53 P
51808
Patent, Dorothy Hinshaw
Dolphins and Porpoises: $14.95

DISCARD